Among The Daffodils

Written by
Carrie Hughes

Among The Daffodils

Inspirational Poetry
By
Carrie Hughes

ISBN: ISBN: 979-8-218-62599-3

Acknowledgements

I would like to express my gratitude to my husband, Kevin, and my son, Davey, whose support has been my guiding light through this journey. This book is as much yours as it is mine.

To my parents, though you are no longer with me, your love and wisdom continue to guide me every day.

A special thank you to my amazing TikTok family. Your encouragement means the world to me. I'm so grateful to each one of you who has been a part of this journey with me.

Introduction

Every poem tells a story and brings us on a
journey to encourage, strengthen, and show
us that there is always hope.

Join me on this journey through my poetry
collection, where we inspire, uplift and find
strength through all of life's moments—
together.

Table Of Contents

Among The Daffodils

She wandered about climbing hills.
She found a perfect place
among the daffodils.
Where their light radiated in the morning sun.
She made wishes for everyone.

The flowers grew beneath the trees.
Sending their love with the morning breeze.
Their golden light was lovely and new.
While blooming in gardens
and dancing for you.

Her happy place made her smile.
Where she'd love to dream once in a while.
She wandered about and loved climbing hills.
She found peace among the daffodils.

Chapter 1

Echoes Of Winter

Winter shares its beauty, and in its magic, time stands still—reminding us to always take time to rest, reflect, and embrace the stillness in life.

"Echoes of Winter" captures the stillness and soul-searching we often feel during winter, using the season as a metaphor for emotional reflection, longing, and quiet moments of growth.

Among The Daffodils

Hello Winter

Hello winter—morning comes fast.
Fall days never seem to last.
Extra blankets to keep me warm.
Hoping for another snow storm.
Branches sway in snowy delight.
Children shout, "let's have a snowball fight!"
A cozy cottage wrapped in snow.
Trees are bare, covered in its glow.
Mornings bring a chill in the air.
Frost is glistening everywhere.
The sun rises to start the day.
It's always hard to get on my way.
Can't wait for hot cocoa tonight.
As the snow falls, what a pretty sight!

Hello January

Hello January…
It's a brand-new year.
A fresh start we hold dear.
New resolutions, hope fills the air.
We let go of the past and leave it there.
As the stars shine gracefully at night.
They gently fade in the morning light.
Cold air brings a chilly start to the day.
Mittens and coats as we go on our way.
The time when dreams begin to start.
The spirit of a new year lives in our heart.

A Part Of You

If I could remember every moment, I would.
If I could hold onto it all, if only I could.
Time moves on.
Things change and grow.
People we love,
may become people we used to know.
Memorize it all, every memory.
Hold onto it tight too.
Because all of it, the good and bad—
is all a part of you.

Alone In The Forest

Alone in the forest, the trees whispered to me.
Touching my soul and setting me free.
Where dreams filled my soul inside.
I found the perfect place to hide.
Alone in the forest where secrets live.
Its power and grace have so much to give.
Where I found hope, deep in its glow.
There's wisdom there I long to know.
Alone in the forest, the trees whispered to me.
Touching my soul—at last, I am free.

Before I Sleep

It's cold and dark, but peaceful too.
It's a quiet night, I have so much to do.
Everything moves a little too fast.
Some days, I wish I could make time last.
The morning light brings calm to the air.
Gentle winds and sweet sounds, everywhere.
Days go by with memories to keep.
I have so much to do before I sleep.

Tattered Wings

Her tattered wings dance through the night.
Hoping with each day she'd be alright.
The haunting whispers softly play.
Shadows fall behind as she walks away.
With each step, her wings begin to heal.
Her courage and strength allow her to feel.
Her tattered wings dance through the night.
Hoping with each day she would be alright.

The Heart Yearns

I don't know, do you?
What is a lie?
What is true?
"Shhh… listen—open your heart."
Watch as the melodies begin to start.
Don't ever lose sight,
of all that is right.
Many twists and turns,
as your heart yearns.
A soul that is lost—
really is quite the cost.
I don't know, do you?
What is a lie?
What is true?
"Shhh… listen—open your heart."
Watch as the melodies begin to start.

Still She Was Brave

She was brave.
Her heart filled with sadness.
She watched the world fall into madness.
Still, she was brave.
She felt anguish all around.
While her peace was shaken and bound.
She was brave.
She stood in the shadows of darkness too.
She was surrounded by light from you.
Still, she was brave.
Because that's all she knew how to do.

Dark Of Night

I hear whispers through the dark of night.
The woods awaken in its peaceful light.
I wander beneath the moon's soft glow.
Where thoughts come alive,
and begin to grow.
I see the beauty in each tree.
It feels as if they speak to me.
In this quiet moment I can hear.
A mystery that I hold so dear.
For a brief moment, there's peace in sight.
As I wander beneath the stars at night.

Star-Crossed

I wait under the stars' soft glow.
I question—
how many things I'll never know.
I look out at the infinite sea.
I wonder, what do you want from me?
My heart is beating so fast as I wait.
I begin to wonder, why are you so late?
Yet still, I wait under the stars' soft glow.
Wondering how many things I'll never know.
Hope fills me as I look at the stars tonight.
Star-crossed forever in the morning light.

This December Day

The warmth of summer is long gone.
Fall has faded away.
The morning air is chilly,
on this December day.
Flurries of snow gently fall to the ground.
I listen for birds, but there's not a sound.
Mornings are quiet.
Seasons change their face.
Birds fly away to find a much warmer place.
If only I could be like a bird at winter time.
I'd find the perfect place and make it all mine!
The warmth of summer is long gone.
Fall has faded away.
The morning air is chilly,
on this December day.

Her Cage

Within the chaos no one saw her at all.
While they were dancing.
No one noticed her fall.
Amid the noise and endless sound.
No one saw the cage she had bound.
In the silence, still, no one noticed her.
When she spoke—she caused quite a stir.

A Snowy Day

A snowy glow gently covers the trees.
A chill fills the air with the morning breeze.
Little crystals, so fluffy and white.
Fall from the sky in pure delight.
A blanket of white feathers,
covering the ground.
It's so magical, not even a sound.
The streets are wrapped in a winter white.
Little kids giggle at this wintery sight.

A Walk In The Woods Late At Night

A walk in the woods, late at night.
Eerie sounds give quite a fright.
Gentle wind fills the misty air.
Snowflakes are dancing everywhere.
Trees shiver beneath the moon-lit sky.
Snowdrifts gather as she walks by.
Alone as her thoughts begin to roar.
Her tender soul begins to soar.
Stars shine like diamonds—a tender light.
What a lovely walk in the woods at night.

A Wintry Night

Walking through the woods on a wintry night.
There's a chill in the air.
Its glow is quite bright.
All the hustle and bustle of Christmas is near.
This quiet time alone, I hold so dear.
In the stillness I feel His loving embrace.
His light shines all through this place.
Trees gently sway within the breeze.
Stars light up the ground with such ease.
Angels dance in shadows on the ground.
In the distance, the sweetest howling sound.
Walking through the woods on a wintry night.
There's a chill in the air.
Its glow is quite bright.

Good Night—
Good Morning

Good Night…
She sits in the dark, gazing at the sky.
So many thoughts keep passing by.
Haunting dreams keep her awake at night.
Hoping for just a glimmer of light.
But the sun has now fallen fast asleep.
Left with many promises still to keep.
Birds are quiet, not making a sound.
As the clock slowly goes around.
The moon begins its long wait.
Morning is what we anticipate.
Soon the sun will begin to shine.
All of this moment will be mine.
Good Morning…

Snowflake Kisses

Snowflakes whisper a soft melody.
Snow gently falls, oh so tenderly.
Branches dance in snowy delight.
Snow angels begin to take flight.
Smells of cookies fill the air.
Hot cocoa and marshmallows everywhere.
The chill of snow kisses my face.
Wonder surrounds this lovely place.
A garden of snowflakes flutters by.
Little kisses falling from the sky.

Silent Night

Silent night, cold and dark.
A haunted moon dims the night.
The soul lies still in the quiet.
As mysteries awaken its light.
Stars drift in the darkness.
Performing its lovely show.
Sleeping away the hours.
Under heaven's nightly glow.

On The Edge

The edge of life can be an empty place.
Isolated—lost in time and space.
Don't look back as time moves on.
You may not remember when the day is done.
She stands alone, unaware of the noise.
She's hoping to capture all the joys.
Sometimes they slip away and fall.
You wish for a moment,
you could forget it all.
The edge of life can be an empty space.
Fear and joy etched forever on her face.

When Life Gets Hard

When life gets hard, walk away.
Kick some leaves, take time to play.
Drink coffee, enjoy simple things.
Watch what joy it all brings.
Take walks, clear your mind.
Spend time in nature, what peace you'll find.
Feeling lost and too tired to fight.
Hand it to God and you'll be alright.

Yesterday's Song

Yesterday, a sweet and bitter song.
Lives in me, I carry it along.
As its weight begins to show.
I choose what I allow to grow.
I let it play over and over again.
I skip a few beats that I want to end.
Even though I left it behind.
Some melodies play within my mind.
Each note takes its own place.
As it wears a bit on my face.
As each day keeps moving along.
Yesterday sings, a sweet and bitter song.

On And On It Goes

Simple was the life she chose.
As each day passes, on and on it goes.
Like a flower in the wind—
falling to the ground.
It finds its way back to where hope is found.
Her soul opened to sounds, so sweet.
Making her life finally feel complete.
Simple was the life she chose.
As each day passes, on and on it goes.

Chasing The Past

I am forever chasing the past.
You'd think I'd run, but I want it to last.
What if I could just try.
When light reaches the sky.
Precious moments to share.
When magic was everywhere.
In the blink of an eye.
It all just flashed by.
It became memories I used to know.
So many memories, they just overflow.
Not that I'm not happy now.
Just wishing, somehow.
If I could go back to see.
Times that were happy for me.
Like being a child, for hours I'd play.
My first kiss, or my Wedding Day.
The most beautiful moments I'll ever know.
When your child's born—
watching them grow.
Special times laughing with a friend.
Wishing those moments would never end—
but then they do.
Before you know it, it's all behind you.
I'm forever chasing the past.
As I get older—it moves way too fast!

If We Fall

I had a dream, I held it in my hand.
As it was coming true, it didn't go as planned.
It's ok because a dream is just a wish, a hope.
You mold it, you let it grow.
You give it a little rope.
When it shows up, the magic is real.
You let go and embrace how you feel.
As we let go, new dreams will pass by.
If we fall, it's ok, we just give it another try.

Worry

Worry sits beside me.
It follows me where I go.
I keep pushing it away, I don't want to know.
Beauty is powerful when worries fade away.
Dreams come alive when worry has no say.
It chases me, tries to drag me down.
I won't let it pull me to the ground.
Worry sits beside me every single day.
I won't let it stand in my way!

Once Upon A Time

Once upon a time…
There was a girl who felt lost,
unsure of where to go,
and what would be the cost?
She wandered around aimlessly for quite a bit.
Turned down a few roads,
realized they weren't it.
The more she roamed,
the more she began to fear.
What if she never finds it?
What if she chooses wrong from year to year?
One day, she was quiet and decided to sit still.
She started to listen, as her heart began to fill.
The answers came in a whisper, a gentle light.
She was ready to hear it.
She knew she'd be alright.
Shhh… listen to what your heart has to say.
It will guide you and help you find your way.
Shhh… listen.

Broken Wings

When we feel lost—
like a bird with broken wings.
We still try no matter what each day brings.
Time moves slowly, as days pass by.
It takes all you have not to cry.
With love, patience, and so much more.
In time—
your broken wings begin to soar.

Chaotic

The world is spinning.
No one is winning.
It's so chaotic.
Almost hypnotic.
Drowned-out voices.
Too many wrong choices.
Life keeps everyone busy.
Feeling lost and a bit dizzy.
Teetering on the edge of a cloud.
Wanting to speak up, but not allowed.
It's so chaotic.
Almost hypnotic.
The world is spinning.
No one is winning.
Teetering on the edge of a cloud.
Wanting to speak up, but not allowed.
It's so chaotic.
Almost hypnotic.

The Shadows

She had dreams once.
Her eyes filled with stars.
They'd come to life—
Strumming on her old guitars.
She waited and hoped they'd come true.
She wanted it more than she even knew.
But some dreams she had to let go.
The reasons she may never know.
Some days when life becomes sad.
She remembers the dreams she once had.
If only she could make everything right.
Sometimes the shadow hides her light.
She pushes it away and lets hope grow.
Even though some dreams she had to let go.

Words On A Page

Thoughts surround her everywhere.
Whispers deep in the night are always there.
Mornings filled with shadows of the night.
Her soul keeps longing for the light.
Words scattered on every page.
Left little pieces filled up in a cage.
As each piece was torn apart.
There's a chance for a new start.
Little pieces gathered up and flew away.
A gift of hope for you to cherish each day.

Where Stars Hide

There's a place where stars hide,
deep in my soul.
Waiting to shine their light.
Like memories on a scroll.
Once I'm brave enough,
to step out into the light.
I can feel it in my heart, it's within my sight.
All I have to do is let the stars do their thing.
And watch the magic the light will bring.
Each star grows as bright as the morning sun.
The light shines as a guide for everyone.
Once I'm brave enough,
to step out into the light.
I can feel it in my heart.
That's when I know—I'm alright.

A Quiet Moment

Take a moment and sit with me.
What do you hear, what do you see?
Birds singing the perfect song.
Don't mind me while I sing along.
Sounds of leaves in the wind.
Maybe I'll dance or just pretend.
A quiet moment to just let go.
There's nothing else you need to know.
Just allow the peace inside.
No need to talk, I'll be your guide.
Take a moment and sit with me.
Close your eyes and simply be.

Spellbound

I feel lost.
Waiting for answers that never seem to come.
I look around—
as if someone's hypnotized everyone.
I feel alone.
Yet so many walk by me every day.
I try to speak, but I don't know what to say.
Words seem too simple,
like a needle without a thread.
If only love could last forever,
but it drifts away instead.
Twilights fate fills the shadows,
as if the world's cast a spell.
The moon and stars dim—
but hope still has secrets to tell.

Hope Whispers "I'm Here"

The music plays from long ago.
A melody only she will know.
Haunting sounds fill up inside.
She tries to face, but rather hide.
Secret tales buried within.
A hope that might have been.
But withered in the night sky.
Haunted by a secret lullaby.
Powerful winds touched her soul.
She fell into its empty hole.
Fate comes to take away.
Secrets gathered along the way.
As hope whispers, "I'm here."
"Come with me, please don't fear."
Still, music plays from long ago.
A melody only she will know.
As hope whispers, "I'm here."

Along Comes One Day

Dreams can break apart,
fall to the ground.
You pick them up
and hope every piece is found.
You hold them, cherish them,
and you believe.
A dream worthwhile
takes so much to achieve.
You hold it in your heart and watch it grow.
You're willing to learn
anything you need to know.
You hope it doesn't get lost along the way.
Then—along comes one day.
Magic happens right before your eyes.
Life hands you an amazing surprise.
Dreams, maybe, just maybe—
along comes one day.
We hope it didn't get lost along the way.

A Bird With A Broken Wing

A bird with a broken wing falls to the ground.
He looks for help, but there's no one around.
He tries to fly away with his broken wing.
He tries to call out but he can't sing.
He takes a moment and a deep breath or two.
He tells himself, "There's nothing I can't do."
He decides to try with only one wing.
His faith grows stronger.
He begins to sing.
He moves a little slower,
but he knows that's ok.
He can move a little bit, at least for today.
As the day goes on he continues to try.
With one wing he believes—
that's when he can fly.

Here We Go

Here we go.
Another month, time keeps rolling along.
We get up singing the same old song.
The stars keep shining till late at night.
Birds are singing in the morning light.
Days are busy while we're running around.
Shhh... do you hear the sound?
The sound of life comes too fast.
Before we know it our life has passed.
Still, I wake up with hope every day.
I take a few moments to always pray.
I hear God's love day and night.
Letting me know I will be alright.
Shhh... Do you hear the sound?
The most loving I have ever found.
I hear it in the flowers that I see.
And when the birds are singing to me.
I hear it in the wind as the trees sway.
I feel it in the sunlight throughout the day.
Shhh... Do you hear the sound?
It's life—as it goes round and round.
Here we go.

A Flower In The Wind

She lost him—somewhere along the way.
He lost his voice. There's nothing left to say.
Echoes of an old forgotten song.
Haunted nights wondering what went wrong.
Like a feather softly falling to the ground.
Floating in the wind never making a sound.
Moments that are slowly drifting away.
A hopeful heart wanders through the day.
Pieces of a love she once knew.
A tender heart broken in two.
Shadows of a past she used to know.
Like a flower in the wind—
she doesn't want to let go.

As You Say Goodnight

If I could leave just one thing behind.
A dream from the past.
The most precious kind.
The sweetest flower,
that blooms a love you once knew.
Nestled between the leaves
and the morning dew.
A star that dances under the moonlight.
A loving kiss as you say goodnight.
If I could leave just one thing behind.
My love would be there waiting—
for you to find.

Candle In The Night

Each tear told a story
of who she used to be.
Moments she held close.
Yet wanted to set free.
The moon lit her heart.
Like a candle in the night.
While hope filled her soul.
In the morning light.
Memories from the past—
of dreams she once let go.
As hope danced in the shadows.
The universe whispered, "hello."

When Stars Fall

Shadows fill the night.
Yet a hopeful heart lives forever in its light.
The enduring soul—
writes their name in the sky.
Dreaming of love without questioning why.
While voices in the dark slowly drift behind.
It's the eternal heart—
that hope will always find.

A Little Crumb

Everything's spinning and I feel numb.
Hope's fading but leaves a crumb.
Do you feel it too?
If I could escape like in a magic show.
I feel it slipping away, but I won't let go.
Do you feel it too?
I reach for the stars, but they're too far away.
The sun wants to shine,
but life gets in the way.
Do you feel it too?
Shadows fall behind as the sun begins to rise.
Leaving behind a little crumb—
as a sweet surprise.
Do you feel it too?
Shhh... please don't make a sound.
See the light dancing around?
Do you feel it too?
It's hope—whispering to you!

The Sun Shines The Next Day

Wind and rain come in the dark of night.
You search, but there's no one in sight.
You realize you are on your own.
It's the saddest feeling I've ever known.
The water takes all your things away.
Yet the sun still shines the next day.
Time stops as you long to cry.
In silence, you're left to wonder why.
And though you lost nearly everything.
You awake to hear the birds still sing.
The sun rises and the sky is still bright.
Hope arrives with the morning light.
As you rebuild, you learn to let go.
You find strength you didn't know.
The path may be hard along the way.
But hope lives on with each new day.

She Was Ordinary

She knew she was ordinary,
simple and plain.
The stars shined within her,
yet no one knew her name.
She was ordinary.
A shadow of her mind.
Sweet reflections
of those she left behind.
She was ordinary,
but she didn't seem to care.
In the silence of her heart.
The sun shined everywhere.
She was ordinary.
A quiet unspoken light.
Hidden within her eyes—
that glistened in the night.
She knew she was ordinary,
simple and plain.
The stars shined within her,
yet no one knew her name.

Secrets In The Wind

Can you hear it?
The wind is so far away.
Its mystery haunts the night.
Whispering softly through the day.
Can you feel it?
The wind as it gently flows.
It touches deep in my soul.
With all the wisdom it knows.
Can you see it?
The wind begins to sigh.
The universe holds all its power.
And its secrets never die.

A Quiet Place

Shadows fill her heart,
with thoughts she can't let go.
They touch her weary soul,
a place she's come to know.
She yearns to understand,
feelings buried deep inside.
But when the darkness falls,
she finds a place to hide.
A quiet place—
where words no longer need to be.
Deep within her soul,
where she can finally be free.
Beams of heavenly light,
wrap her in its glow.
Whispering to her soul—
it's time to let go.

She Dances In The Shadows

She dances in the shadows,
with secrets she never told.
Her heart beats at night,
shielding her from the cold.
Silent whispers fill her soul,
with memories that faded away.
When life felt simple,
so different from today.
She gazes at the moon,
bathing in its love and light.
As it casts its spell, somehow—
she knows she'll be alright.
She dances in the shadows,
with secrets she never told.
Mysteries of a time and place,
where dreams never grow old.

The Sun, Moon & Stars

The sun goes to sleep in the night.
Dreams tenderly dance, what a lovely sight.
Teardrops fall as the moon hides its glow.
While singing its song to those below.
Heaven's hands reach out for you to hold.
Shielding your heart from all the cold.
Stars flicker gently hoping for light.
Whispering softly, "You'll be alright."

Like Diamonds On The Water

Like diamonds on the water,
sparkling in the night.
Silence fills the shadows, hiding from its light.
A weary dream rests on a cloud's soft wing.
Waiting in hope
for love the sun will bring.
Birds singing eternal hymns of love.
As God's light pours His grace from above.
Like diamonds that shimmer,
in the dark of night.
Her heart overflows with love—
from His tender light.

Mysteries Of The Night

Mysteries of the night fill the sky.
With no answers we wonder why.
We look for an angel's gentle hand.
To guide us so we understand.
We danced beneath the moon's glow.
Whispering secrets to those below.
We wait with hope in the morning light.
For truth to awaken in the night.
Mysteries of the night fill the sky.
With no answers we wonder why.

Chapter 2
The Promise Of Spring

Spring awakens the soul as birds sing,
reminding us that hope will always come after
a long night.

"The Promise of Spring" captures the
resilience found in nature, bringing subtle yet
powerful transformations that can happen
when we least expect it.

The Place Where Hopes And Dreams Grow

She has a secret,
she holds close to her heart.
Filled with hopes and dreams,
the place where wishes start.
At night she visits her dreams
and holds them close too.
She believes with all her heart,
someday they'll come true.
When the time is right,
that is when she will know.
For now, they sit inside her heart,
the place where hopes and dreams grow.

Where The Fairies Grow

There's a magical place where fairies hide.
A tiny garden you can find outside.
They love to dance with butterflies.
And sing the sweetest lullabies.
They sparkle and shine in the night.
And love to hide in the morning light.
Their dainty wings help them fly.
Touching flowers while fluttering by.
The little fairies stay out of sight.
Only little ones can see their light.
A dreamy place, not for all to know.
A hidden garden, where the fairies grow.

A Sweet Butterfly

A sweet butterfly opens his wings.
I feel all the magic he brings.
I watch his beauty as he takes flight.
His soul shines with love and light.
He flies with grace through the air.
I smile as he touches me with care.
He flutters about on his way.
I hope he comes back another day!

A Spring Symphony

We waited for this moment to finally see.
The beginning of a Spring symphony.
Birds wake up singing the loveliest song.
I dance with butterflies and sing along.
Orange blossoms bloom all over its trees.
Flowers surrounded with cute little bees.
Days grow warmer and longer too.
New plants grow, the sun smiles at you.
My soul is touched,
as I watch this beautiful sight.
Spring begins and our hearts take flight.
I smile as a new Spring shows its face.
With each new flower, hope gives us grace.
We waited for this moment to finally see.
The beginning of a Spring symphony.

Hello Hope

With each season, change is here.
Joy surrounds us year to year.
Fireplace cuddles on a winter night.
Spring brings hope in the morning light.
Long summer days are always sweet.
Ladybugs and flowers, what a treat!
With the start of each new fall.
Hope reminds us to treasure it all.

All of Life

All of life, there is beauty and pain.
The sun always shines after each rain.
As seasons change, a new song will play.
It brings lovely melodies along the way.
New beginnings, bring hope with its light.
Tender whispers heard through the night.
The heart grows through it all.
Winter, Spring, Summer and Fall!

A Daffodil—
It's The Sweetest Kind

Hope begins with each new spring.
What joy the daffodils will bring.
They bloom a love tender & sweet.
Surrounding trees along the street.
They grow for just a little while.
And stand tall with grace and style.
The most perfect flower you'll ever find.
A daffodil—it's the sweetest kind!

Her Wings Of Hope

A little bird perched on my windowsill.
As I awaken, the air is warm and still.
I wonder what message she'll bring today.
Her eyes are soft as she glances my way.
Her wings of hope, gracefully sway.
Her melody's sweet, as she flies away.

Dance Of The Butterflies

My garden grew lovely and bright.
Where butterflies would dance, a lovely sight.
One landed right on my knee.
He just kept looking up at me.
I thought it rather curious though.
What is it he wanted me to know?
I watched as his wings gently swayed.
Up and down the flowers, they played.
I smiled and watched their magic show.
So peaceful, hoping they wouldn't go.
What a sweet moment in my day.
Just like that, they flew away.
I kept dancing and decided to wait.
For wings of grace to show their fate.
Each new morning, to my surprise.
A lovely dance of the butterflies.

Within The Trees

The sun smiles through the trees.
Its light radiates with such ease.
Reminding me in the morning light.
Somehow, everything will be alright.
It's quiet, so graceful and free.
I breathe it in, as if it's all for me.
I feel it all, a loving embrace.
A tenderness, its roots hold in place.
A sound so peaceful, a perfect sight.
Its soul touched me in the morning light.
There's magic here, it's everywhere.
Within the trees—as I was standing there.

Her Magic

I see magic.
It's all around.
Can you see it?
Shhh…
Don't make a sound.
Can you feel it?
I feel it too.
It's everywhere.
Shhh…
Her dreams are in view.
Can you touch it?
Her enduring soul.
Shhh…
Move softly.
Her heart takes a toll.

The Poetry Of Life

She walks through her garden,
touching each flower.
She breathes it all in and feels all their power.
Chattering birds sing to her a lullaby.
While butterflies gracefully dance by.
The trees whisper a lovely sound.
One of the most peaceful she's ever found.
It's a mystery how it reaches this place inside.
Where magic lives, but likes to hide.
Thoughts fill her soul with light.
As they begin to take flight.

A Bird's Song Of Hope

A tiny bird perched on a little tree.
He looked up at me so peacefully.
Oh, how he made the sweetest sound.
As he playfully flew round and round.
He gently swayed his little wings.
I smiled from all the joy he brings.
I watched his lovely tender dance.
Happy to see this moment by chance.
He moved softly through the trees.
Building his nest from twigs and leaves.
His feathers kept him warm at night.
He sang of hope in the morning light.

The Visit

A sweet bird flew by, perched high in a tree.
I listened with wonder, as he sang to me.
His voice was gentle without saying a word.
It was the sweetest sound I've ever heard.
He touched my soul,
I watched him, carefree.
As if he were performing on a stage—
just for me.
As a feather began to fall,
I wished he would stay.
But as quickly as he came,
he decided to fly away.

Wings to Fly

She walks through clouds.
With an incredible light.
Her smile shines—
letting them know she's alright.
It fills her soul as she lights up the sky.
Allowing her to heal as she learns how to fly.
With every breath she feels her heart.
Each piece sewn together,
hoping they won't fall apart.
She walks through the clouds.
She lights up the sky.
She spreads her wings—destined to fly.

Greet The Day

Another day goes by.
The sun comes up, birds still fly.
I wonder what today will be?
Hope fills the air so tenderly.
I watch the sun gently rise.
Today will be its own surprise.
Birds greet the day with lovely song.
I pray with hope and sing along.
The sound of joy fills my heart.
As a new day begins to start.
As another day goes by.
The sun comes up.
Birds still fly—and so do I.

Tiny Blue Feathers

Sitting by my window on this lovely day.
I heard a voice whisper.
"How are you today?"
Much to my surprise and awe.
The cheeriest bird I ever saw.
He smiled and made the sweetest sound.
As he circled up and all around.
He perched and bathed in the morning light.
His tiny blue feathers shined so bright.
I marveled at his playful way.
As he took a bow and flew away.

Left Behind Pieces—
A Mother's Soul

For my mom …

Her soul left behind pieces for me.
I feel her in everything I see.
A tenderness that comes through the day.
Pieces of her heart that were allowed to stay.
I carry it with me everywhere I go.
A peace that I am lucky to know.
I hear her voice in the bird's sweet song.
I see her smile as butterflies dance along.
When I'm still and allow myself to hear.
The sounds of whispers, I know she's near.
She's a part of everything I see.
Her soul left behind pieces for me.

He Wore Bright Red Feathers

God sent a bird with a message today.
He wore bright red feathers.
What would he say?
He whispered softly a sweet melody.
As if an angel was singing just for me.
I was comforted by his loving wings.
Peace filled my soul with the joy he brings.
He lifted his wings up to the sky.
Heaven touched my heart—
as he waved goodbye.

Flowers Dance

In the morning while the flowers dance.
Each new day brings another chance.
We start fresh with the morning dew.
A world of possibilities are waiting for you.
Each day's a gift, wrapped in the sun's glow.
With endless opportunities for us to grow.
As the beat of flowers continues to sway.
We're blessed with another beautiful day.

The Tiny Seed

Simple and free is the life she chose.
She lives each day—and on it goes.
Like a tiny seed with faith, it can grow.
The sun and rain are all it needs to know.
Gently it grows when watered every day.
It begins to blossom as it finds its way.
A flower in the wind falls to the ground.
Somehow—
it finds the place where hope is found.
Like a flower, as her soul grew.
Her life found its meaning too.
Simple and free is the life she chose.
She lives each day—and on it goes.

The Place Where Hope Grows

She was lost and broken, her soul empty too.
Trying to decide what path to take,
unsure of what to do.
She saw roads ahead,
wondering which one to take.
Hesitating, she didn't want to make a mistake.
She started down a road.
It just didn't feel right.
She quickly changed directions,
with a new path in sight.
There were many ups and downs,
all along her way.
She decided not to give up,
at least not for today.
With many twists and turns,
she found a place no one knows.
Buried deep within her heart,
the place where hope grows.

Among The Earth

The earth knew who I was meant to be.
It could feel every breath of me.
It gave me lessons I needed to know.
Planted seeds and watched them grow.
I danced among the stars' loving light.
The moon brought wisdom with the night.
I sat beneath a tree, its roots held in place.
The wind came, and brought its loving grace.
The sun whispered, "Come follow me."
As my soul opened, it set my spirit free.
The earth knew who I was meant to be.
It could feel every breath of me.

Peekaboo

After winter melts away.
A flower begins to find its way.
A little seed nestled in the ground.
The sweetest gift of love we found.
While it sleeps in the dark of night.
It plays peekaboo in the morning light.
It begins its story for all to see.
It brings joy along so tenderly.
As a new flower starts to show.
Hopes and dreams begin to grow.
With a bow from the sunlight's ray.
A new flower has found its way.

In The Morning Light

For a brief moment in the morning light.
Sweet bunnies dance as birds take flight.
The morning sunlight begins to shine.
All this beauty that surrounds me is mine.
Birds sing to me a gentle prayer.
I feel the Lord's blessings everywhere.
For a moment, I breathe it all in.
Before the world begins to spin.
The morning sings me a quiet song.
As I begin my day, I hum along.

The Meadow

I found a meadow when I was young.
Made of songs waiting to be sung.
Filled with hopes, dreams, and wishes.
I picked one and closed it tight—
gave it lots of kisses.
Held onto it, treasured it through time.
Waiting—
hoping for the day I could call it mine.
Somedays, I still visit the meadow—
and bask in the sun's glow.
Because hope never stops.
It only continues to grow.

What would you choose?

Gardens Of Kindness

Give your love out to the world.
Shine your beautiful light.
Enjoy your journey,
don't give up the fight.
Plant seeds of kindness
everywhere you go.
Watch as gardens of kindness
continue to grow.
Keep shining,
smile throughout your day.
Be a guide for others,
help light their way.

The Perfect Home

I gaze up to the sky, so serene.
The trees, a beautiful bright green.
The sun's rays softly peek through,
as if it's gently hugging you.
Whispering secrets of a forgotten past.
Sounds of another life that didn't last.
Scattered leaves drift with the wind.
For a moment, I sit and just pretend.
Nature and my soul become one.
I'm completely embraced by the sun.
The wind stops spinning too fast.
For a moment though, it doesn't last.
The breeze returns with elegant grace.
Sounds fill up this beautiful place.
A tiny garden I made my own.
Even though it's a bit overgrown.
It's mine, as I sit here all alone.
I finally found, the perfect home!

Finding Happiness

Happiness can't be bought; it can't be found.
It's not in the things you like to have around.
It's not in the light from the morning sun,
or a gift given to you from someone.
Happiness isn't a thing you hold—
there is no guide.
The only place you'll find it—
is by looking inside.

My Kingdom On Top Of The Hill

In the middle of this busy town.
There are paths that wind up and down.
My Kingdom hides atop the hill.
Come climb with me. I hope you will.
A place where butterflies like to go.
Where birds perform a lovely show.
The flowers dance as you walk by.
Wild blueberries grow, don't think I'll try.
Sit for a while in its loving grace.
Breathe in peace that fills this place.
Take some home and let it be.
I'm happy you took this journey with me.

Let's Take A Stroll Through The Neighborhood

Let's take a stroll through the neighborhood.
We can walk together, I think you should.
Notice all the things there are to see.
I'm glad you're walking here with me.
Walk through cul-de-sacs where children play.
Wave to neighbors as you go on your way.
Be sure to turn down a different street.
There's a new neighbor you'll want to meet.
Watch little squirrels climb up a tree.
I know butterflies are dancing just for me.
The sky is clear, crystal blue,
as if the heavens are watching over you.
Flowers surround houses on each street.
Leaving behind a fragrance, so sweet.
Little bunnies hopping all around.
Listen, do you hear every sound?
Cars going by, up and down.
There's so much joy in this lovely town.
Look around, do you see?
The magic that's surrounding me.

Among The Flowers

For my mom …

I remember your voice and your lovely smile.
I close my eyes
and think of you once in a while.
I see you among the flowers—
dancing on a cloud.
I wish I could be with you,
but I'm not allowed.
I hear you singing with angels,
a lovely sound.
The sweetest butterflies
are dancing all around.
You look happy, at peace, and free.
For a moment, I felt you close to me.
There's the most beautiful love,
surrounding you with light.
In this moment, I know I will be alright.
I left you among the flowers,
dancing on a cloud.
I wish I could have stayed—
but I wasn't allowed.

The Willow Tree

As each seed is planted,
the willow tree will grow.
Filled with wishes and dreams
you long to know.
It lives in the meadow, rooted in grace.
Its leaves gently sway,
holding dreams in place.
Branches bring shade to all who sit below.
A magic hideaway where children love to go.
Raindrops fall softly.
The willow begins to weep.
A message so tender, it holds within, so deep.
Its soul is alive as its heart flows in the wind.
It touches the ground—
as the weeping willow grinned.

The Little White Chair

The little white chair sat alone.
Surrounded by trees that had overgrown.
Many people would come and go.
Holding secrets only a garden would know.
The scent of flowers filled the air.
Statues overlooked with tender care.
An angel statue stood nearby.
A blackberry tree—maybe I'll try.
Snuggled in trees on each side.
Hidden gardens, the best place to hide.
A glimpse of a table nestled by a tree.
I found the perfect place to inspire me.
A lovely garden, filled with secrets there.
I imagined it all—
as I sat in the little white chair.

The Little Hummingbird

The little hummingbird stopped by one day.
Oh, how I wished that he would stay.
He flew near a bush in my garden bed.
Cuddled blossoms by the old wooden shed.
He danced with the flowers—
humming a lullaby.
He sipped sweet nectar until it ran dry.
He played in branches that fell on the ground.
While I sat and enjoyed this lovely sound.
As he began to fly away.
Oh, how I wished he would stay.

The Little Bunny

The little bunny comes at night.
When everyone's sleeping and out of sight.
She watches through our window with care.
Wondering about the family living there.
Her little white tail wiggles with glee.
She always hides when she sees me.
With the cutest long ears and white fluffy tail.
She hops through the yards
and down the trail.
Searching gardens for food in the day.
Hopping from lawn to lawn on her way.
The little bunny is the sweetest thing.
She loves to visit us every spring.

In the Meadow

In a meadow far away.
Flowers bloom while butterflies play.
I touch each flower and feel their light.
There's a misty dew left from the night.
For just a moment I closed my eyes.
Waiting for the morning sun to rise.
I feel Each flower's peaceful touch.
I dream a little, I worry too much.
Wildflowers dancing carefree.
Putting on a show just for me.
It's time for me to go on my way.
Flowers seem to want me to stay.
I feel each flower's peaceful touch.
I dream a little, I worry too much.

There Was A Little White House

There was a little white house
that sat near the bay.
Surrounded by roses
where my son used to play.
I can still hear his giggles
as he ran through the yard.
Though we've moved on,
leaving was hard.
Rooms were filled with voices,
many from the past.
If only time could stand still—
and moments could last.
We built our hopes and dreams in each room.
We planted our garden and watched it bloom.
The loveliest swans danced in the bay.
Barbecues were many on a warm summer day.
The winters we bundled up, oh, the snow!
It was hard to leave when it was time to go.
A house is ours to hold with care.
Until a new family will live there.

The Place Where Dreams Grow

Come with me—
to a place where dreams grow.
Where stories are told from long ago.
Where wishes grow on fairy wings.
Enchanted by all the wonder it brings.
Where a princess and prince find true love.
Where clouds of hope dance high above.
Through the forest and off we'll go.
Away from everything we know.
A place where magic waits for you.
The land where fairy tales come true.
Come with me—
to a place where dreams grow.
Where stories are told from long ago.

Carrie Hughes

My Soul Inside A Flower

I planted flowers in my garden
and watched them grow.
Watering every day,
I couldn't wait to say "Hello!"
I placed a piece of my soul
inside of each one.
Hoping a little light
would bring love to everyone.
Each flower bloomed
under the sun's loving light.
Dancing as the wind—
whispering through the night.

The Rhythm Of Life

Tree branches reach toward the sky.
Singing their love as leaves drift by.
Some fall softly to the ground.
Whispers echo as hope is found.
A life filled up inside this tree.
Touches my soul with its mystery.
The light shines with secrets to hold.
So many are lost, as roots grow old.
While the wind sings a perfect melody.
The rhythm of life plays music just for me.

Sweet Little Daisy

Sweet little daisy, loved by the sun.
A simple gift, shared with everyone.
Sweet little daisy, delicate and free.
Whispering her joy dancing tenderly.
Sweet little daisy, shares her loving light.
Filling our hearts with pure delight.
Sweet little daisy, a love only she knows.
We wait, as the little daisy grows.

Fancy Is The Rose

A sweet breath of hope
has finally arrived.
The sun whispered its glow,
that's how she survived.
Music stirred her soul,
filling her with light.
Grace poured its love,
through the starry night.
Deep love and sorrow
whisper as they collide.
Fancy is the rose—
that's hidden deep inside.
Her eyes told stories
from so long ago,
of a heart beating,
dreaming of its glow.
A sweet breath of hope
has finally arrived.
The sun whispered its glow—
that's how she survived.

Hope Within A Daisy

As the daisies dance,
my heart is carefree.
With each breath I take,
I know they're talking to me.
They speak of love
that touches the place.
Where hope finds its light,
filling me with grace.
As the daisies dance,
light fills the skies.
Hope within a daisy—
brings a joyful surprise.

His Charming Ways

The little bird flies from tree to tree.
Singing of a love that's meant to be.
His tiny wings move with love and grace.
Bringing hope to this tranquil place.
I smile with wonder at his charming ways.
He brings me joy with melodies he plays.
He rests his weary head beneath the sky.
While he sings to me the sweetest lullaby.

Little Bird, Little Bird

Little bird, little bird,
nestled in a tree.
Rest your little wings,
stay close here with me.
Little bird, little bird,
will you sing a song?
Your momma is here.
I'd love to sing along.
Little bird, little bird,
as you learn to fly.
Momma's by your side.
It's your time to try.
Little bird, little bird,
with your cheerful smile.
Momma is here.
Stay with me, just for a while.
Little bird, little bird,
Will you talk to me today?
Momma's here with you.
Please don't fly away.

Where Wildflowers Bloom

Her smile is a light that touches the sky.
She loves to dream watching clouds go by.
Her heart is a garden
where wildflowers bloom.
The sweetest love that fills every room.
While melodies dance, singing a lullaby.
Her dreams blossomed—
watching clouds go by.

The Sun Whispers

The water glistens softly,
as the wind tenderly blows.
Filling her soul—
with all the secrets it knows.
The sun whispers its love,
across an endless sky.
Echoes of hope fill the night,
as her dreams begin to fly.
Mornings bring inspiration,
a longing from the night.
She dances with hope,
bathed in radiant light.

Serenity

There's a field where she loved to hide.
Filled with flowers stretched far and wide.
They whispered the sweetest lullabies.
She made wishes watching the sun rise.
The shadows danced in the sun's glow.
With each wish new flowers would grow.
Where birds would sing joyous songs,
she found the place where she belongs.
A place of dreams where she was free.
Her secret place—pure serenity.

Butterfly's Journey

A beautiful spirit fills our soul.
Wings of beauty, majestic and whole.
Sweet moments soaring wild and free.
Dancing for us so tenderly.
Beneath the sun's warm, golden light.
The butterfly's journey is pure delight.
Whispering songs of hope and grace.
Resting on flowers, their quiet place.
Carrying messages within their wings.
What a joy their lovely presence brings.

Among The Daffodils

Chapter 3
Breath Of Summer

Summer reminds us that after each storm, the sun will always begin to shine again. Summer days bring joy and laughter even after the dark, reminding us that the light will always shine in our hearts.

"Breath of Summer" captures the resilience and warmth that follows life's storms, while celebrating the enduring joy and light that summer brings.

Dreams

Dreams may come and dreams may go.
The reasons why, we may never know.
Some dreams hide deep within.
Unspoken wishes, waiting to begin.
If you can hold your dream in sight.
Watch with wonder, as it takes flight.
Dreams may come and dreams may go.
If we don't try, we'll never know.

A Day At The Beach

Take my hand and walk with me.
Feel the breath of an endless sea.
While the sun shines through the day.
For a moment, let's drift away.
Watch seagulls dance in the sky,
as colorful kites are floating by.
Collecting shells along the sea,
a perfect treasure just for me.
Feel the sand beneath your toes.
Watch as each wave gently flows.
A day at the beach, the perfect way.
To find some peace and drift away.

Where The Light Shines

Do you feel the shift in the air?
Magic stirring, I sense it everywhere.
Do you see a door opening,
filling us with light?
While our hearts find peace—
everything's alright.
Do you hear it, a peaceful sound?
Touching our souls where hope is found.
In this moment, we're meant to be.
Where the light shines, we're finally free.

Come With Me

Come with me…
Get lost in the magic of the night.
Peace is found in the soft moonlight.

Come with me…
As melodies begin to play.
Get lost in stars along the way.

Come with me…
The soul awakens like the morning sun.
Radiating its love through everyone.

Come with me…
Take my hand, let's go.
Watch as dreams begin to grow.

Come with me…
Get lost in the magic of the night.
Where peace is found—you'll be alright.

Simple Days

We lived in a time of innocence.
The days were simple and sweet.
We had no idea how lucky we were.
Growing up then was such a treat.
I remember the long days of summer.
All the kids played together outside.
We played games in the churchyard.
It always had the best place to hide.
We walked for hours with no place to go.
There were things then we didn't know.
We spent hours outside just to play.
The world seemed so far away.
Peace was felt all through the night.
You just knew everything would be alright.
A time we were all innocent and free.
We had no idea—
what changes our world would see.
We lived in a time of innocence.
The days were simple and sweet.
We had no idea how lucky we were.
Growing up then was such a treat.

Can You Hear The Music Play?

There's a place where time stands still.
In those moments, I believe it always will.
Can you hear the music play?
Each moment has its place along the way.
Flowers grow among the weeds,
even the ones with tiny seeds.
Some rise up, incredibly tall,
while others never grow at all.
Sounds of love fill the air.
Some are no longer there.
I can hear the music play.
Some moments lost along the way.
Yet I still hear the sweetest sound.
The most precious one, I've ever found.

Dance With Me?

For my dad …

Would you like to dance one more time?
This moment, it's just yours and mine.
Let me take you by the hand.
I'll hold you and help you stand.
One more dance—you and me.
Let the music set you free.
One more dance—just you and me.

Hey Little Bird

Hey little bird—
I don't want to chase you away.
I wanted to say hello.
You make my day.
You flew by, found a spot right by me!
I'm smiling, watching you be so free.
The sounds you make, serene and sweet.
I listen intently—it's quite a treat!
A moment before life gets in the way.
I wish it could last forever,
I wish you could stay.
Hey little bird—
I don't want to chase you away.
I wanted to say hello before I start my day!

As The Birds Dance

In the morning with the dawn.
I open my window to bird song.
The sun rises with a new day.
Birds wake up and begin to play.
They dance from tree to tree.
One even seems to notice me.
His tender eyes glance my way.
While his feathers gently sway.
I reach out to touch his wing,
as he began to gently sing.
I feel as though I'm in a trance.
I watch as birds gracefully dance.
Peace fills the morning air.
Birds are dancing everywhere.

Happiness Is A Gift

Happiness is a gift we give with each smile.
When we're happy, life feels more worthwhile.
We wish each day could be a happy one.
Sending love and joy to everyone.
Happiness is hope on a dark rainy day.
The love we feel each time we pray.
Happiness comes from deep inside.
When we're able to open our hearts wide.
Happiness is always yours to find.
The easiest way is to simply be kind!

Wander

I love to wander,
feel the grass beneath my feet,
watch the sunrise—it makes my life sweet.
I walk on the beach and stare at the sea.
As if each wave rolls perfectly for me.
I watch as clouds gracefully go by.
I smell flowers, their scent fills the sky.
I sit in my garden; bird song fills the air.
Peace and joy surround me everywhere.
I love to wander,
feel the grass beneath my feet,
watch the sunrise—it makes life complete.

Let's Build A Happiness Tower

Build a happiness tower.
Fill it with all your power.
Take all the chaos that you see,
wrap it up, hand it to God, let it be.
Fill your tower with a peaceful theme,
ready whenever you need to redeem.
Fill it with joy and let it overflow.
Watch magic begin and happiness grow.
When life becomes too hard to bear.
Remember, your tower is always there.
Watch it grow and shine bright.
When life is hard, sit in its light.

Sweet Dreams

Sweet dreams.
Angels will be your guide.
Hug the clouds.
They'll take you on a ride.
Stars will light up a magical show.
Imagine all the places you can go.
Spread your wings, fly over the sea.
Climb mountains, enjoy its mystery.
Surround yourself in peace and light.
Sweet dreams—have a good night.

Cottage By The Sea

She lives in a cottage by the sea.
Watching the waves flow gently.
She hears children giggling as they play.
Collecting seashells throughout her day.
She stands where the tide and beach meet.
Smiling as water caresses her feet.
Her floppy hat sways in the breeze.
The waves roll to shore with ease.
She almost falls into its roar.
Laughing, craving more and more.
At night, the sun goes to sleep.
While the ocean's light glows deep.
The sea's power calms with the night.
Then awakens again in the morning light.

Hidden Magic

Hidden magic is everywhere.
I won't tell—I wouldn't dare.
It's for you to try and find.
Look ahead and look behind.
It's hidden, not easy to see.
Yet somehow, it calls to me.
I see it with open eyes.
Every day a new surprise.
Whatever you do—don't blink.
It'll be gone, or so I think.
Open your heart and let it through.
The magic is there, waiting for you.

Summer Days

Summer days are lovely and sweet.
Gazing at the sea is always a treat.
Building castles and angels in sand.
Carefree moments, nothing is planned.
The scent of salt fills the air.
The sounds of summer everywhere.
Magic rays of sun on my face.
I feel peace in this magical place.
As I watch, waves gently go by.
My soul lights up and begins to fly.

The Ocean

The ocean is made to survive.
Something inside me comes alive.
I watch each wave caress the shore.
Leaving me longing more and more.
I embrace its mysterious ways.
Falling into the melodies it plays.
Alone with myself and all I dream of.
Magic fills my soul with its tender love.

June Arrives

June takes its first breath in the evening light.
All of nature awakens to a lovely sight.
The hum of bees circling flowers is sweet.
The sound of crickets, like a faint drumbeat.
Leaves on all the trees shine bright.
Flowers blooming in the daylight.
The sun is shining through each tree.
I marvel at the lovely gifts I see.
Pure gratitude fills my soul today.
I feel your presence, guiding my way.

Sunshine

In the morning, stillness fills the air.
A gentle breeze shines light everywhere.
Birds sing the loveliest morning tune.
While she dances beneath a sleeping moon.
Happiness awakens with the morning sun.
Her heart and sunshine become one.
A tender soul now ready to fly—
becomes one with the morning sky.

An Ordinary Sweetness

She was ordinary—
A life filled with moments simple, yet sweet.
Walking with grass beneath her feet.
Her heart embraced the morning sun.
Watching the moon dance as the day is done.
Nights spent gazing at an endless sky.
As days and nights go drifting by.
In the silence she found destiny here.
An ordinary sweetness she holds dear.

In The Clouds

She danced with the morning sun.
Surrounded by flowers freshly spun.
She searched for clouds floating by.
Jumping up as if she could fly.
The sweet breeze was her guide,
as her wings took her for a ride.
She floated by gentle flowing streams.
She felt her heart within daydreams.
As she slowly drifted away.
She knew she wasn't able to stay.
She danced beneath the stars' gentle light.
Embracing their love as she shined bright.
As she circled round and round.
　　She knew—
This is the place where happiness is found.

Finding Peace

I looked outside trying to find,
the perfect place for a peaceful mind.
Is it in the sun that shines bright?
Is it in the stars that glimmer at night?
Is it in your smile that I seek each day?
Is it in the words I speak when I pray?
Is it in the flowers, so perfect and divine?
I kept looking outside, but I couldn't find.
The peace I'd searched for so long.
Was inside my heart—all along!

The Little Ladybug

I watched as the cutest little ladybug flew by.
She snuggled the flowers—
played hide-and-seek with a fly.
She opened her wings, and I hoped she'd stay.
I smiled as I realized she wanted to play.
She hugged all the flowers
and settled near a tree.
She kept moving around.
I think she's teasing me.
Just as I had hoped she would stay.
I watched as the little ladybug flew away.

My Red Camaro And Me

Turn the key in the ignition,
let the eight-track play.
A 76 red Camaro,
cruising the highway.
Sun shining down,
singing my favorite song.
Dancing in the car
while friends tag along.
A car made for dreams,
as I grip the wheel tight.
Pounding on the gas
as I take off at the light.
What memories I have,
I was young and carefree.
Cruising along—
My red Camaro and me!

Turn Right Off Of Park Street

Past the plaza,
turn right off of Park Street.
There's a charming house,
and a family I'd like you to meet.
The house sat next to the church,
where all the kids would play.
There lived a little girl,
who was quiet and loved to pray.
Dad was a police officer.
He loved to tell stories and dance.
Mom worked at the school.
Our dog Mandy loved to prance.
I was the youngest of three,
a brother, a sister,
and then there was me.
Alone in my room
with the record player on.
Hairbrush in my hand,
singing my favorite song.
The driveway was always
the best place to play.
I'd put Mandy in a baby carriage
and we were on our way!

A few blocks from there
was a neighborhood park.
I'd make dreams in the rose garden
until it was dark.
I'd hang out at the railroad tracks.
They seemed to go on for days.
It was such a different time,
in so many ways.
All the neighbors were loving and sweet.
How lucky I was to grow up—
on this beautiful street.

Little White Clouds Of Joy

She sipped cappuccino on a hot summer day.
Watching people come and go,
she chose to stay.
She breathed in the aroma, bitter yet sweet.
With little white clouds of joy—
her favorite treat.
How about a dash of cinnamon
on top just for you.
Don't forget,
you must add a pinch of sugar too!
She sat beneath red umbrellas, cup in hand.
Enjoying this moment, perfectly unplanned.
She sipped cappuccino on a hot summer day.
Watching people come and go,
she chose to stay.

Castle In The Sky

Stairs went on forever to our castle in the sky.
Driving over the causeway,
watching summer days go by.
Magic castles made in the sand,
as they washed out to sea.
My brother catching bluefish,
my sister riding the waves with me.
Summer at the shore—always a special treat.
Shhh… mom's sneaking to A&W.
for root beers across the street.
Surf City had custard, too many flavors to try.
There was a local diner,
chocolate chip pancakes, oh my!
A beautiful lighthouse,
we always went there.
I can still hear the seagulls,
hermit crabs everywhere!
Long Beach Island—the summer place to be.
Some of my loveliest memories—
always waiting there for me.

Her Little Red Wagon

I remember playing in the yard
when the days felt so long.
Pulling my little red wagon
with Mandy tagging along.
She was a tiny white poodle
with a yappy little bark.
We played outside for hours
staying out until it got dark.
When that familiar song played
we knew the ice cream truck was near.
It's probably why summer
was my favorite time of year.
Our yard stretched so far.
The sky was always blue.
No clouds in sight—
more special than we knew.
My Uncle loved to stop by.
He loved to hang out.
"Carolyn, it's time to eat,"
my momma would shout!
Mandy nipping under the table
at my uncle's feet again.
I treasure all the memories
from way back when.

I remember playing in the yard
when the days felt so long.
Pulling my little red wagon
with Mandy tagging along.

This Fine June Day

Take my hand and walk with me.
What wonderful things we will see.
It's early on this lovely day.
Let's get lost along the way.
There's magic in the morning light.
Watch flowers bloom in pure delight.
Let the grass tickle our toes.
Feel its peace as the wind blows.
Listen to birds' sweet-sweet song.
Oh, the butterflies—let's dance along.
We'll talk about our hopes and dreams.
Make flower bouquets beside streams.
Come with me this fine June day.
Get lost with me along the way!

A Place I Once Lived

I remember a special time,
when things were simple and sweet.
Memories of a place I once lived,
where trees lined every street.
Flowers bloomed in each yard.
Children played outside all day.
You could hear the sweetest sounds
of laughter as they'd play.
Summer days, sitting on the grass,
watching butterflies go by.
Being amazed at the simplest things,
like pretending I could fly.
Sundays were always special—
off to church we'd go.
We'd play for hours,
waiting for our favorite TV show.
It was a special time,
when things were simple and sweet.
Memories of a place I once lived,
where trees lined every street.

The Sea Whispers

As waves gently roll, they pull me in.
Reminding me of places I've never been.
Its power stays long after I'm gone.
Like a picture so tenderly drawn.
Whispers of love that's meant to be.
A longing inside when I'm by the sea.
My arms reach out and feel its touch.
Memories of a sea I love so much.
I feel its secrets as it draws me in,
and hold onto hope, till we meet again.

A Place To Rest

There's a place to rest near a tree.
The sounds become a part of me.
The wind holds onto me so tight.
My soul rests in all its light.
It whispers love and surrounds me.
My perfect place, beneath a tree.
The branches reach up toward the sky.
I sang with birds as they flew by.
I watched ducks dancing in the lake.
A moment in time that's mine to take.
As life keeps moving by so fast.
I breathe it in and make it last.

Songs Of Summer

Songs of summer play by the sea.
Singing, "come take a walk with me."
Each wave begins to take flight.
Dreams are found in its loving light.
Filling your soul with love and grace.
Sweet kisses from sun on your face.
The waves continue to gently flow.
It holds secrets I long to know.
The songs of summer continue to play.
Take a walk with me this lovely day.

Above The Clouds

Her weary heart gazes at the sea.
She whispers, "are you looking for me?"
His loving hand reaches to her below.
Filling her with wisdom she needs to know.
Darkness fades with the morning sun.
Her soul fills with love for everyone.
Above the clouds and the deep blue sky.
Her graceful wings are ready to fly.
Blessings written in her dreams today.
Filled with love, she'll gladly give away.

Her Cottage On The Lake

Her cottage on the lake,
where cypress trees grow.
A perfect place to dream
and watch nature's show.
Surrounded by trees,
water reflects heaven's light.
Her soul awakens each morning,
embracing this lovely sight.
Sounds of heavenly music
from birds in the sky.
With all of its mysteries,
she watches life pass by.
She places all her dreams
deep inside its light.
As she waits—
she knows she'll be alright.

The Old Shining Sea

I found a glimmer of light,
by the old shining sea.
It was all it had to give,
the only piece for me.
Its light filled my soul,
as wisdom grew within.
Waves cradled the shore,
in a place I'd never been.
Shadows filled the sky,
stars gleamed in its light.
The ghost of past memories
drifted through the night.
As heaven began to whisper,
"Come and sit with me."
Shhh... listen, as waves go by,
the old shining sea.

Watching The Ducks

She found peace by the lake one day.
Watching as ducks went on their way.
The sun shined its beauty within its light.
She knew at that moment, she'd be alright.
As they went by whispering love and grace.
She knew she had found the perfect place!
She found peace by the lake one day.
She watched the ducks move along their way.

Dreamy Eyes

Dreamy eyes imagine the perfect place.
While the wind blows gently on her face.
Away from chaos that's everywhere.
Do you want to meet me there?
Butterfly wings take us on a journey far away.
Where sunlight dances with joy
all through the day.
Birds lift us up with the loveliest song.
Come with me—we'll sing along.
Flowers bloom forever in its light.
Peace and calm surround the night.
The sounds of love fill the air.
Light radiates with tender care.
Dreamy eyes imagine the perfect place.
While the wind blows gently on her face.

Do You Know?

Do you know?
Do you see the world spinning all around?
Yet you stand still, not making a sound.
Do you hear the birds singing to you?
Do you dance with butterflies too?
Does the wind touch your soul
with every breath?
Do you wonder what happens after death?
Do you feel God's love throughout the night?
Do you find peace with Him
in the morning light?
Do you know the power you have each day?
When you're kind
to those you meet along your way.
Do you know?
Oh, I hope so.

By The Lake

I sat by the lake one September day.
Captivated by its charm, I chose to stay.
I felt it pull me in like never before.
As if in a trance, I could feel its lore.
I saw my reflection staring back at me.
Secrets so hidden that only I could see.
Whispers from long ago played in my mind.
Memories of a past that I left behind.
I was sitting by the lake one September day.
Shadows of a time I've kept hidden away.

My Grandpa And Me

If I close my eyes, I can see.
A special memory of my grandpa and me.
Just the two of us walking along.
He was humming his favorite song.
A memory I hold forever in my mind.
A moment when he was gentle and kind.
He walked me to school one sunny day,
and paused a moment along the way.
He asked people ahead—
"Do you mind if we pass?"
They stepped aside and waited on the grass.
They smiled and you smiled back too.
Such a precious memory I have of you.
We continued along our way.
I never forgot the memory of that day.

Dance By The Sea

Will you meet me by the sea?
In the quiet, waves talk to me.
Stars cast their loving glow.
So many secrets I long to know.
The sea touches the night sky.
No need to worry or wonder why.
Just hold my hand and dance with me.
Let the ocean hum you its melody.
The moonlight leaves its love behind.
A peaceful heart is ours to find.
Are you ready to take a chance with me?
Let your dreams dance by the sea.

If Only She Could Grow Wings

She would dream of so many things.
If only she could grow wings.
She'd fly like a bird through the trees.
As worries faded away in the morning breeze.
She would dance in the sky,
where she could be free.
While the wind whispered secrets—
of what could be.
She'd wander through clouds
without a care at all.
She knows the wind will catch her if she'd fall.
She would dream of so many things.
If only she could grow wings.

A Tiny Grain Of Sand

Walking while watching the tide roll by.
Dreaming of love,
where the sea meets the sky.
Dancing on crystals, a tiny grain of sand.
Waiting, will she ever understand?
Clinging to hope, will her dreams come true?
In her heart—
she's always been dreaming of you.
Crystals grow old, piercing like nails.
Was her heart just spinning fairy tales?
Collecting crystals one by one,
dreaming of hope for everyone.
She danced on crystals, mere specks of sand.
Maybe one day she'll finally understand.

Among The Daffodils

Chapter 4
Whispers Of Fall

The magic colors of fall fill us with love,
letting us know that faith will come with the
autumn breeze.

"Whispers of Fall" captures the beauty found
in the changing colors of autumn, bringing
comfort and peace, even as things transform
around us.

Hello September

Hello September.
Summer says goodbye,
with a sweetness all its own.
A time for new beginnings—
the loveliest I've known.
August takes its bow with love and care,
while squirrels are scurrying everywhere.
Leaves begin to turn and fall to the ground.
While robins sing the loveliest sound.
Busy mornings, school buses everywhere.
The aroma of apples begins filling the air.
Though September always arrives too soon.
We wait to dance under the harvest moon.
The tender breeze reminds us fall is near.
The beauty of change—September is here.

The Wrap Around Porch

Rainy days I found the best hideaway.
I would write stories there about my day.
It was a secret place near the big oak tree.
With a wrap around porch made just for me!
I giggled at butterflies that I loved to chase.
I have so many memories of this lovely place.
I loved to dance and sing my favorite song.
While animals in my story would sing along.
There was a rainbow forest that came alive.
A magical lake where I watched dolphins dive.
The cutest baby monkeys who never grew.
The sweetest birds who danced—
and could talk too!
I almost forgot,
a little unicorn who loved to give kisses.
Of course there was a genie
who granted all my wishes.
I built a world where my fairy tales came true.
It was the most amazing place I ever knew.
So many tales that I loved to write about.
Stories that were so silly, I have no doubt.
It was a place that always made me smile.
I go back in time to visit once in a while.

Beyond Today

If we knew what was coming,
we'd turn the other way.
No one chooses the hardest road—
or knows beyond today.
Each path we take,
is a journey of up and down.
Sometimes twisting us in directions,
we wish we could turn around.
As we move through life,
our shadows move behind.
Up ahead the unknown,
you don't know what you'll find.
Keep an open heart and let it guide your way.
No one chooses the hardest road—
or knows beyond today.

Hurricane

It comes with the wind; life's not always fair.
Like walking a tightrope—
with no time to prepare.
Powerful and fierce, it moves fast.
Hold on tight, I promise it won't last.
As you journey through life,
you may trip and fall.
Hold on tight,
remember to give it your all.
Because in the end, that's all you can do.
Faith and hope will carry you through.

Grandma's Meatballs

Can you smell the aroma?
Grandma's meatballs, oh my!
I can almost taste them—
though many years have gone by.
Always mixing up the dough,
ravioli, yes please.
I'll have a second helping—
no pasta with peas!
Sunday dinners,
homemade sauce on the table.
Kids playing, life was simple.
We didn't even have cable!
Those were the days,
at least that's what grandma said,
when it cost less than a dollar—
just for a loaf of bread.
Mmm… that aroma.
Grandma's meatballs, oh my!
I can almost taste them—
though many years have gone by!

The Little Rocking Chair

In the dusty old attic where I loved to play.
Sat a little rocking chair by the window bay.
At night, in the quiet, the little rocking chair.
Rocked back and forth, but no one was there.
Shhh… "Can you hear it?"
My brother would say.
I never heard it when I'd go up to play.
A creaking sound could be heard—
all through the night.
It was always silent in the morning light.
I believe an angel would always stop by.
Rocking back and forth, humming a lullaby.
Shhh… do you hear it, sometimes at night?
Rocking back and forth—
until the morning light.

A Moment From My Past

For my mom ...

Her voice was like an angel
that carried through the house.
I hid on the stairs
and stayed quiet as a mouse.
The sound of her singing,
always made me smile.
I like to go back in time
and visit once in a while.
She loved to dance.
Her smile radiated light.
She always let me know
I would be alright.
She was always happy
when she sang and dreamed.
I loved those moments,
how perfect they seemed.
I hold them in my heart.
I hope they last.
When time stood still—
a moment from my past.

The Same Old Ride

Every day, we continue the ride.
No matter how hard you want to,
we can't hide.
As you look out the window,
the past keeps going by.
Flowers grow tall,
while some grow weak and die.
Some grow strong,
filled with hope that grows.
Some get lost along the way—
and the struggle shows.
Some build themselves a meadow—
with love and care.
Some stand-alone,
wondering why no one is there.
Yet still, we all continue the same old ride.
No matter how hard we want to,
we can't run and we can't hide.

Chasing Her Dreams

She loved to dream on her old metal swings.
When she was young,
she imagined so many things.
Her heart filled with hope
as she reached for a star.
She sang songs she wrote
on her favorite guitar.
She wondered, "What will my future be?"
While sitting, writing beneath the old oak tree.
Would she be picking flowers
in the morning sun?
Or strolling for hours, praying for everyone.
Would she be dancing under moonbeams?
Or spending the days chasing all her dreams.
She loved to dream on her old metal swings.
When she was young,
she imagined so many things.

Used To Be

Once there was a girl with stars in her eyes.
Every day felt like a new surprise!
I remember her, she never felt alone.
She had a smile and a life all her own.
There are always moments,
they hit me some days.
It affects me now in so many ways.
So many memories of the girl who used to be.
She wasn't wild and crazy,
but she was always free!
She loved each day.
She had hopes and dreams too.
Sometimes I even forget
the plans I had for you.
Life had a way
of finding the right place for me.
But there are moments I remember—
the girl I used to be!

Following My Heart

Looking in the mirror,
there's many faces I can see.
Some are in the distance,
some stare back at me.
I see the past in my reflection—
struggles in eyes looking my way.
I'm trying to find my way in the world
and what places I should stay.
The roads haven't been easy—
not sure what direction my life should go.
Sometimes I climbed mountains and
questioned when I didn't know.
Sometimes I've fallen down,
thinking there are things I can't do.
Afraid to face the future,
and obstacles from which I withdrew.
I'm still staring in the mirror,
only now I can see the light.
I see myself as I am now—
knowing that I'm alright.
I'm following my dreams,
no longer afraid of the unknown.
I'm hopeful with how far I've come
and how much I've grown.
Now I see far away in the distance,

someone smiling back at me.
She's peaceful and happy,
she's where she wants to be.
She's following what's in her heart,
being all she can be.
Now as I look back in the mirror—
that's my future that I see!

Looking Up At The Moon At Night

Surrounded by stars and its loving glow.
Radiating light to those below.
Dreams dance under a celestial sky.
While the tides are softly drifting by.
Clouds are drifting all around.
In the stillness, there is no sound.
God's love shines throughout the sky.
The moon takes its bow as the sun passes by.
It gives light to the sky and sea.
Its wonder always fascinates me.
My heart awakens to a lovely sight.
Looking up at the moon at night.

"Where Is The Moon" She Asked?

"Where is the moon?" she asked.
Maybe it's silly, though.
Is it catching dreams—
while performing its nightly show?
Maybe it's dancing,
moving all around in space.
Waiting for a silver lining,
surrounded by its grace.
While the stars glow
in the beauty of its light.
It shines its love forever,
through the dark of night.
I wonder where the moon would be—
If it was dancing, just for me?

November Has Arrived

November has arrived
with beauty and grace.
Before the cold comes,
morning frost shows its face.
Piles of leaves line the streets.
Night skies bring a full moon.
Days become shorter.
Holidays are coming soon.
Fires begin to burn
and warm houses at night.
It's time to be thankful—
November arrived with delight.

Being Your Mom

I saw you first—from that moment I knew.
My soul is touched forever by you.
I've watched you grow each and every day.
So much wonder as you learn and play.
Time moves on, way too fast.
So many moments I wish could last.
Being your mom, watching the days go by.
While you spread your wings and begin to fly.
I saw you first—that's the moment I knew.
My soul has been touched forever by you.

Leave Behind

Leave a little kindness
wherever you go.
Happiness and hope
are only sure to grow.
As you journey through life,
every single day.
Leave behind some gratitude
and joy along the way.
Leave a little love
and some compassion too.
You may bring happiness
to someone you never knew.
As you're going along,
a surprise just for you.
What you leave behind—
comes right back to you!

Dear Younger Self

Dear younger self…
Would I teach you
all the wisdom I have today?
Would I show you mistakes
I made along the way?
Would I give you more
of unconditional love?
Would I give you my all
so you'd know you're enough?
Would I feed your soul
with the strength to succeed?
Would I warn you of all the traps
of failure and greed?
What would I tell my younger self?
Oh, if only I could.
There's so much beauty
I wish I had understood.
Each day is a moment—treasure it all!
Live with your heart, it's ok to fall.
Reach for strength, find your own light.
You are growing and learning,
never lose sight.
Who you are is a choice you make every day.
Choose wisely—let your heart lead your way.

Hope's Tender Kiss

Her heart was weary,
as though it might break.
It filled up her soul, leaving a profound ache.
Hope's tender kiss touched her late that night.
As she prayed, her soul embraced the light.
When morning came, light filled her mind.
In letting go, weariness was left behind.

Only A Spark

Show the world your smile,
no matter what life will bring.
Always remember to laugh,
don't worry about anything.
Life is too short to carry stress
through your day.
All it really does is just get in your way.
Real peace comes from a place within.
It only takes a spark for peace to begin.
Show a little kindness in all that you do.
Before you know it—it comes back to you!

More Than Gold

Her smile was lost among the trees.
It lights up shining in the morning breeze.
Carefree, she runs along the sand.
Knowing that few will understand.
A life well-lived is worth more than gold.
She'd rather run than stand still and grow old.
Sunlight brings warmth to her aching soul.
As she watches each wave endlessly roll.
That's how she knows she's alive and free.
It's the only way she knows how to be.

Carrie Hughes

The Joy Of Autumn

Can you feel it?

Fall arrives with its autumn breeze.
While acorns fall from atop the trees.
Leaves turn shades of yellow and brown.
Letting go as they gently fall to the ground.
And as leaves stand in the morning light.
God's beauty shines on us so bright.
Coffee by the lake makes mornings sweet.
Snuggling in sweaters is always a treat.
Warm blankets and apple pie too.
Spending evenings cuddled up with you.

Turn The Lock

I'm putting the past inside a box.
With tiny bows and little locks.
Filled with memories,
you know the ones I mean.
We want to forget and wish we'd never seen.
I know it's time to let it all go.
Like a withered flower,
that can no longer grow.
I tie a little bow and lock it away.
With grace—I turn the lock today.

The Part That Happiness Brings

I used to know her, a little girl full of light.
Her smile could chase away
even the darkest night.
I forgot who she was and who she used to be.
That little girl who still lives inside of me.
Many summer days I never wanted to end,
laughing and holding hands
with my best friend.
Whispering secrets that only we knew.
So many random thoughts
shared between us two.
It's funny how time goes on and we forget.
We tend to focus on the things we regret.
I'm learning to let go and forget those things,
and hold onto—
the part that happiness brings.

Round and Round

She watches.
She notices—
when no one else will.
The world's spinning round and round.
Yet she stands—perfectly still.
She hopes no one notices.
She doesn't want the world to see.
She's clever, hiding her real identity.
She's kind, she cares too much.
She hides behind her shadow
where no one can touch.
The world keeps spinning round and round.
Yet she stands—perfectly still.
She notices—
when no one else will.

Life's Lessons Along The Way

Close your eyes,
let your heart guide your way.
Mistakes are only lessons
you may experience each day.
Life has many twists and turns
that can lead to despair.
All you need to do
is place it in the Lord's care.
When the road is bumpy
and fear embraces you so.
It's the Lord reaching out
and teaching you to grow.
All of life's lessons
you experience each day.
Are the Lord's guiding hands,
helping you on your way.

Maybe She's Sensitive

Some say, she just doesn't try.
Maybe she's sensitive, and a little bit shy.
She waits and waits for a glimmer of hope.
Moment after moment, trying to cope.
She wears a pretty dress and a perfect smile.
She even lights up the room once in a while.
No one notices that it's all just pretend.
She holds it inside—
waiting for the moment to end.
She feels more than her heart can bear.
She wishes somewhere, someone would care.
She can sense everything—all of it too.
As if she hears thoughts
coming right from you.
Her instincts are powerful
right from her soul.
She's sensitive; it takes quite a toll.
So many feelings—too many to know.
She carries it with her but wants to let go.
Some say, she just doesn't try.
Maybe she's sensitive, and a little bit shy.

How You Danced

For My Dad ...

Oh, how you danced—
your eyes would light up.
Watching you, I couldn't get enough.
You danced with such style and grace.
How I adored your lovely face.
Oh, how you danced, so loved and admired.
Watching you, I couldn't help but be inspired.
You held my hand with a spin and a twirl;
I felt as if I was a little girl.
Oh, how the music would bring you to dance.
If only you were here and we had the chance.
I'd take your hand with a twirl and a spin.
Watching you laugh with that silly grin.
Oh, how he danced and made it his own.
For now—she dances alone.

"Will You Marry Me?"
He Asked

"Will you marry me?"
he asked on a mountaintop.
She said yes, and life came to a stop.
I was lost in your eyes, my heart beat so fast.
Was this moment really meant to last?
To have and to hold, to love and cherish too,
as we build a life we love—
I want to grow old with you.
"Will you marry me?" he asked so long ago.
Forever and always—
our love continues to grow.

Never Forget

No matter how much you stumble and fall.
Never forget to embrace it all.
You are worth it and will get through.
You'll learn, grow, and get stronger too.
Never forget, this is your time.
You deserve it all. It's time to shine!
Oh, but what if I fall? What then?
You'll catch yourself and try again!

That Night The Storm Came

That night the storm came
and washed it all away.
It left our hopes and dreams,
they were allowed to stay.
The wind became unstoppable,
angry waves grew bold.
The spirit of our town held on
as the raging storm took hold.
Days turned into weeks,
many grew so tired.
With time, spirits renewed,
and our hearts became inspired.
It left us with many lessons,
while our things were swept away.
Stories of unexpected courage—
with memories from that day.

Steps To Happiness

Happiness is just a moment away.
Waiting for the right words to say.
Can you find that place deep inside?
I can help you. Let me be your guide.

Step 1: Let go of worries, release all regret.
This is the step you must not forget.

Step 2: Be thankful for all that you do.
Embrace the best parts of you.

Step 3: Forgive everyone.
It's something you must do.
Don't forget to forgive yourself too.

Step 4: Choose to be happy—feel it inside.
Now it's your turn to be someone's guide.

The Little Mountain

There's a little mountain
where peace can grow.
Teaching you things you need to know.
Where silence has its own sound.
The sweetest breath I've ever found.
Where secrets hide within its trees.
Butterflies and birds playfully tease.
A garden of magic it loves to hold.
I wonder what stories were never told.
The little mountain hides secrets at night.
Whispering—
"Come find me" in the morning light.

If Every Day Of Life Was A Song

If every day of life was a song,
filled with hopes and dreams—
would you sing along?
As the lyrics inspire and set you free.
The stars sing a beautiful harmony.
Drums beat through the highs and lows.
Will you dance with me—
when the music slows?
I'll strum on the guitar in perfect tune.
I'll dance to jazz under the moon.
And as the beat goes round and round.
If my song is silent and loses its sound.
Would you sing the chorus just for me?
Or stop the music and let it be.
If every day of life was a song,
filled with hopes and dreams—
would you sing along?

On My Way To Happiness

I'm on my way to happiness.
Do you want to come along?
Let's forget about our troubles
and whatever's going wrong.
Focus on the good things
that surround us each day.
Fill up on all the moments
that bring joy along the way.
Happiness is in the journey,
not the end of the road.
Believing in the impossible,
even when the music's slowed.
It's like a wave in the ocean,
moving up and down the shore.
The older I get, the more I realize,
I want it more and more!
I'm on my way to happiness.
Do you want to come along?
Let's forget about our troubles
and whatever's going wrong.

While Among The Trees

Mossy trees lined each path as she walked by.
Sounds of fallen leaves
from the ground where they lie.
She stood for a moment.
finding peace in their shade.
Hoping that this feeling would never fade.
She continued down each path
of her lovely walk.
She wondered if the trees could really talk.
What stories would the trees write?
Are secrets hidden beneath their light?
What dreams do they carry
as their roots grow?
A mystery she's always longed to know.
She kept walking down paths, through it all.
While among the trees—
she felt so small.

My Wish For You

I Could Wish Many Things For You ...

I could wish for a fabulous sports car
or fancy clothes for you to wear.
For everything you've dreamed of to happen
and no struggles for you to bear.
I could wish for tremendous wealth,
so you never have to work again.
To be surrounded by nothing but sunshine,
and never feel heartache or pain.
But of all the wishes I could wish,
if I could only wish one thing.
Always believe in yourself,
no matter what life may bring.
Never stop reaching for your goals
or believing in your dreams.
Face each challenge with
courage and strength—
no matter how impossible it seems.
Climb every mountain in your path,
reach for every falling star.
You have so much to offer in life;
always know how special you are.

Always be patient
and understanding of others,
appreciate life in every way.
Always look inside your heart—
and you will always be ok.

Give A Little Happiness Away

Be loving...
We're here to make a mark.
Find someone to love and light a spark.

Be kind…
We're here to help others grow.
To gain the wisdom we need to know.

Be strong…
No matter the battle you have to fight.
He'll guide you and help you make it right.

Have faith…
You may have troubles, reach for His hand.
He'll fill your heart and help you understand.

Be happy…
Choose to find happiness in all that you do.
Don't forget, give a little happiness away too!

A Smile Takes A Journey

A smile takes a journey from me to you.
Hold onto it with care; be sure to share it too.
A mysterious gift,
we never know how far it goes.
How many new smiles are found,
no one really knows.
As a smile wanders,
and drifts from place to place.
It fills each soul with magic—
an infinite light of grace.

The Room With Windows

Once upon a time—
a long time ago.
There lived a little girl
who didn't want to grow.
She lived inside a castle
nestled among the trees.
With a garden of lovely flowers
and dancing little bees.
In a room filled with windows
that circled all around.
She dreamed of a place
where all of hope was found.
A magical place,
where a wish could simply be!
Magic was always hidden
in its own mystery.
Once upon a time—
a long time ago.
There lived a little girl.
I once used to know.

The Autumn Bird Sings

There is a place where the autumn bird sings.
Life begins anew with the joy he brings.
Wishes grow with dreams for tomorrow.
Treasures of hope that we lovingly borrow.
We reach for the clouds that drift far away.
While holding onto love, the gift of today.
There is a place where the autumn bird sings.
Where the hopes of tomorrow—
are found in his wings.

The Sun Will Rise

As the skies turn dark and grey.
Something mysterious is coming our way.
Hope fills the day with gentle care.
The wind twists and turns through the air.
Only God knows where it will land.
We offer prayers and take His hand.
As the sky deepens, dark as night.
In His embrace, we will be alright.
Shadows may linger in the skies.
But in the morning, the sun will rise.

Carrie Hughes

A Tiny Leaf

A tiny leaf within her heart
slowly turns to gold.
Filling her with joy
as she begins to grow old.
A tiny leaf whispers,
"Hope will always grow."
The heart fills with dreams
she once used to know.
A tiny leaf dances
with tenderness and grace.
Love grows in the wind
gently across her face.
Treasures fill her heart
as she begins to grow old.
A tiny leaf fills her soul
as it slowly turns to gold.

We Danced Beneath The Moon

We danced beneath the moon.
I can see your smile.
I like to go back in time every once in a while.
You still make my heart stir.
Do you remember the way we were?
We were so young and carefree.
Oh, the way you looked at me.
Can you hear it, my heart beating fast?
So many memories I wish could last.
Can you still hear the music play?
It feels like it was yesterday.
We danced beneath the moon.
I can see your smile.
I like to go back in time every once in a while.

Beneath The Stars

The ocean holds its power in our hand.
Something we really don't understand.
The moon and earth feel its glow.
Filled with mysteries we don't know.
Though it's deep and dark beneath the sea.
I hear a sound— it's calling to me.
It whispers as waves continue to roll.
A loving sound that touches my soul.
Beneath the stars that shine each night.
With love, it brings magic in its light.
The ocean holds its power in our hand.
Something we really don't understand.

Words Come To Life

Just words on a page,
the best part of me.
Maybe it's the only part
I allow people to see.
Maybe it's a part of my soul
that I hold so dear.
Maybe it's a piece of my heart
I've learned not to fear.
Words come to life,
breaking free from their cage.
They gives meaning to moments
written on each page.
Just words on a page,
the best part of me.
Maybe it's the only part
I want people to see.

The Moon Whispered Goodnight.

She gazed at the moon, standing in its glow.
She became someone she didn't know.
An unspoken wish held secrets unseen.
As she held on, she began to dream.
Her heart was full, embraced in its light.
She felt it pull her in.
As the moon whispered—
"Goodnight."

Wishes On Stars

Wishes on stars fill the sky.
Dreams of hope are waiting to fly.
I always believed it was a matter of time.
I would make all my dreams mine.
They were always there, waiting for me.
To open up and set them free.
As the sound of fate begins to play.
Tomorrow always seems far away.
As the wind gently flows by.
We chase our dreams, at least we try.
In the silence, we can finally see.
They were always meant to be.

Her Dusty Old Guitar

Mornings were a favorite part of her day.
She would take her dusty old guitar
out and play.
She wrote songs about life,
even though she was young.
There were hopes and dreams
in every song she sung!
Sometimes her pain was too hard to bear.
So she built her own castle
and found peace there.
She spent quiet days simply dancing alone.
While writing songs,
dreaming of being grown.
She loved to pray
and put prayers in each song.
She hoped He would hear
and was singing along.
Mornings were always
a favorite part of her day.
She would take her dusty old guitar
out and play.

Hello Fall

Hello Fall...
Whispering its soft glow.
Beauty slowly starts to show.
Leaves begin to turn, singing a perfect beat.
As autumn's breath begins;
summer's goodbye is sweet.
Scents of pumpkin fill our homes.
Let's pick apples for some pie.
Leaves dance round and round,
as if falling from the sky.
Trees are lonely and leafless,
branches sway in the air.
Sweaters warm the soul,
God's love is everywhere.
Chill fills the morning; the sun slows its ray.
Rustling sounds on morning walks—
the perfect fall day!

About The Author

Writing has always been a way to connect and understand the deepest parts of myself and the world around me. With each poem I strive to create moments of reflection and inspiration, hoping to find understanding, while bringing a message of hope and joy into each day.

I hope my love of nature brings comfort, inspiration, or simply a quiet pause in your day. My hope is that my poetry resonates with your soul and inspires you to embrace your own journey.

With love, Carrie Hughes

Among The Daffodils

Poem Index

U